# CAMPING'S LITTLE BOOK OF *WISDOM*

for a clever bear-bagger.
Happy Birthday
Kanchan.

Better read this before
The summer adventures
begin — Shailesh
April 98

# CAMPING'S LITTLE BOOK OF *WISDOM*

*379 indispensable bits of camp lore*

*and humor*

## by David Scott

**ICS BOOKS, Inc.**
**Merrillville, Indiana**

Copyright © 1994 by DAVID SCOTT

**Published by** ICS BOOKS, Inc.
1370 E. 86th Place Merrillville, IN 46410
800-541-7323 / 219-769-0585

10 9 8 7 6 5 4 3 2 1

Printed in the U.S.A.
All ICS titles are printed on 50% recycled paper from pre-consumer waste. All sheets are processed without using acid.

recycled paper

Library of Congress Cataloging-in-Publication Data

Scott, David, 1971-
Camping's Little Book of Wisdom: 379 indispensable bits of camp lore and humor / David Scott.

  p.   cm.
  Includes index.
  ISBN 0-934802-96-3
  1. Camping--Quotations, maxims, etc. I. Title.
GV191.7..S36   1994
796.54--dc 20

                93-48761
                CIP

*To my family, whose love and constant support
have helped weave the loose threads of my life into a band of steel.*

Special thanks to: Dr. William Forgey, for all of the encouragement. ICS books, for having faith in this project. Nicole Villanueva, for putting up with me while this project was in the works. Mark Bonfield, for his longtime friendship and honest advice. Chuck Mohrle, for his wisdom and humor. Buck Tilton and Michael Hodgson for their generous contributions. Rob Tice, for teaching me a great deal of the camping information written in this book. My friends at Indiana Camp, for their support. And, to Scott Power, for teaching me to have faith in myself and my work.

# Introduction

Each and every day, tremendous advances are being made in the world of outdoor equipment. Thanks to modern technology, we now have fabrics that breathe, two-pound tents capable of withstanding 100 mph. winds, sleeping bags that have kept people warm in arctic conditions, and (of course my personal favorite) espresso makers that can be used in conjunction with any good backpacking stove.

All of these remarkable advances allow us to spend our time in the backcountry more comfortably and, in some instances, more safely.

However, with each step forward, we blindly take two steps back. The more we create, and the more we advance, the more separated from the wilderness we become. We tromp into the wilds wearing "Gore-Tex" as our suit of armor, using a tent as our shield, and wielding a trusty walking staff as our sword. We are constantly fighting to protect ourselves from "the elements," when in the process, we lose touch with "the wildness."

No, the purpose of this book was not to persuade you and me to fast, while sitting naked on a glacier in the lotus position, but simply to get back "in touch" with nature. However, while on our quest to climb higher, hike farther, and canoe wilder waters, this book reminds us to slow down, and to remember not only where we are, but who we are as well.

So the next time you head off into the backcountry, don't forget to pack, in your heart, the spirit of the wilderness. And in your mind, a vision of what wilderness, true wilderness, is all about.

1.) Wake up at least every now and then, in time to watch the sun rise.

2.) Learn cooking over an open fire where permitted.

3.) Do your best to enjoy the outdoors safely.

4.) "Minimal impact" means caring.

5.) Make an effort to carry no more than one third of your body weight.

6.) Stay put when lost.

7.) Never purchase poorly made camping equipment; someday you'll be sorry.

8.) Go on night hikes.

9.) Eat before you're hungry and drink before you're thirsty.

10.) Take preventive action on blisters before they take action on you.

11.) Camp out for a weekend by yourself.

12.) Never make assumptions in the wilds.

13.)  Wax or silicone your equipment
      zippers if you have difficulty in
      moving them.

14.)  Don't forget to air out your tent
      after an outing.

15.)  Try cooking with sourdough.

16.) See if you can follow an
animal trail (proceed with
caution if the tracks are
larger than your own).

17.) Never hike with your hands in your pockets while wearing a heavy pack.

18.) Don't let Mother Nature catch you unprepared.

19.) Sit down from time to time.

20.) Set up your tent before going camping to make sure all the pieces are there.

21.) Never use a river as a rest room.

22.) Remember that it is most often better to take thirty steps around an obstacle than three steps over it.

23.)   Marvel at the common.

24.)   Don't be afraid to camp out in a
       torrential downpour.

25.)   Don't camp in a low spot during a
       torrential downpour.

26.) Place a lid on a pot of water while heating (it will boil faster, and save your fuel).

27.) Don't hide from fear, it can be a positive emotion, as well as a powerful teacher.

28.) Always wear your life jacket when canoeing.

29.)   Leave no trace.

30.) Always use direct pressure to stop the bleeding.

31.) Never hike the same trail over and over again.

32.) Don't be misled by believing the better the gear the better the camper.

33.)   Don't be misled by believing
       that the previous lesson applies
       only to camping; it applies to life
       in general.  He who dies with the
       most toys is still dead.

34.)   Wear layers of clothing instead of
       one bulky garment.

35.)  Go on a mountain bike trip.

36.)  Don't camp under rocks or limbs
      that appear as though they may
      fall.

37.)  Please do not  litter; the wild
      lands are a privilege for every
      one, and every thing.

38.) Don't hurry to get from point 'A' to point 'B'. The greatest joys will be found in between.

39.) Never dig trenches around your tent.

40.) Eat foods high in carbohydrates when camping at high altitudes.

41.) Remember to get a physical and have your teeth checked before going on long excursions into the wilds.

42.) Use a windscreen on your stove as often as possible.

43.) Make an effort to follow the "high & dry, smooth & level" rule when setting up a tent.

44.) Don't travel deep in the back-country without letting someone know where you are.

45.) Don't cut green wood for fire wood, gather dead wood.

46.) The perfect campsite is discovered, never created. *-Michael Hodgson*

47.) Practice good hygiene in the back-country.

48.) Learn a few quick release knots for items such as stuff sacks.

49.) Don't head into the bush with thoughts of challenging or conquering the wilderness.

50.) Clean fish down wind and well away from camp.

51.) Make certain your tent is secured even if the weather seems calm.

52.) Don't use stinging nettle or poison ivy as a source of toilet paper.

53.) Take the time to learn basic survival techniques before your next adventure.

54.) Don't break an early
morning silence in the
wilds.

55.)   Watch out for ant hills when
       setting up camp.

56.)   Always pack your share of a group's
       gear.                    —*Buck Tilton*

57.)   Don't use a flashlight when the
       moon is full.

58.) The wilderness can be a harsh place to those who are unprepared.

*—Michael Hodgson*

59.) Buy gear from salesmen with experience.

60.) Never hold your compass next to metal objects unless you wish to walk in circles.

61.) The turtle knows more about the trail than the hare.

62.) Irrigate an open wound until it is thoroughly clean.

63.) Carrying a map and compass is important; knowing how to use them is essential.

64.) Practice dumping or tipping your canoe so you know how to recover before your next outing.

65.) Climb a tree if the urge strikes you.

66.) Never tell your group you feel o.k. when really you don't.

67.) Remember that every pound on your feet equals five on your back.

68.) Don't use a camp stove in a tent
unless you are freezing to death.

69.) Attempt to reach your limits.

70.) Accept your limitations with
humility.          —*Michael Hodgson*

71.) Take time to go skinny dipping in a mountain lake.

72.) Prepare yourself for temporary shock when doing so.

73.) Never carve towards yourself when using a knife.

74.) Wilderness does not care. Experience can be a cruel and heartless teacher.

*—Buck Tilton*

75.) Be aware of beehives when setting up your tent.

76.) Venture as far as your heart and your skill will carry you.

77.) Stop to smell the flowers. But check for bees first.

78.) Don't kill plant vegetation; it's as alive as a bear or a bug.

79.) Never breathe inside a sleeping bag while temperatures range below freezing.

80.) "Answering nature's call" is the only appropriate time to leave something behind—leave it unobtrusively.

81.) Rest and cool off strains and sprains immediately.  *—Buck Tilton*

82.) Separate yourself from the wilderness as little as possible.

83.) Always share your goodies.

84.) Don't put any fuel in a stove that is not specifically designed for that fuel.

85.) Never place trust in any water source. Disinfect—better safe than sorry.

86.) Try camping with small children.

87.) Always live today as if you were to die tomorrow.

88.) Never underestimate the trampling ability of a full grown moose.

89.) Never allow your water filter hose to rest in the sand or mud when filtering.

90.)  Pack out whatever you
      pack in.

91.) Don't forget to stretch before hiking.

92.) Never dwell on your discomforts.

93.) All ice is thin ice—cross only when necessary. —*Buck Tilton*

94.) Gorge yourself with wild berries.

95.) Make certain they are not poisonous!

96.) Take chances with an understanding of, and a willingness to accept the consequences.

97.) Make time for the wilderness.

98.) Let go of worries and they'll let go of you.

99.) Never bathe in a river with soap even if it is "biodegradable."

100.) Never leave food in unsealed, or "smell through" containers when traveling in bear country.

101.) Don't fear being yourself.

*—Buck Tilton*

102.) Don't break park regulations.

103.) Never set up camp on a re-vegetation area.

104.) Store your water bottles upside down to prevent the lids from "ice locking" in cold temperatures.

105.) Roast marshmallows.

106.) Take the time to learn from the animals.

107.) Don't forget to take short breaks on long hikes and to drink plenty of water on each of those breaks.

108.) Every now and then let some of your fish go. (Use barbless hooks.)

109.) Never try to out-climb a bear.

110.) Never try to out-run a bear.

111.) Never try to out-swim a bear.

112.) Never mess with a mother bear
and her cubs.

113.) Don't walk any faster
than the slowest person
in your group.

114.) Watch the night sky for meteor showers.

115.) Always help with duties around camp.

116.) Don't shoot whitewater that is beyond your level of ability.

117.) If your feet are cold, even in your sleeping bag, put on a hat.

*—Buck Tilton*

118.) Follow your heart.

119.) An emergency or survival situation is the only time to break the rules of minimum impact.

120.) Insulate water bottles in a wool sock during cold weather if no other insulator is available.

121.) Don't bother occupied nests, burrows, or dens.

122.) Find a listening point in the woods.

*—Michael Hodgson*

123.) Be careful when putting Deet or any other strong insect repellent above or around your eyes.

124.) Tell ghost stories around the campfire.

125.) Always make sure that your "proper gear" works properly.

126.) Keep your camera handy for a quick shot.

127.) Take lots of pictures.

128.) Because photography is expensive, take good shots.

129.) Let go of time.

130.) Remember at all times that you are but a part of the wilderness not it's ruler.

*—Michael Hodgson*

131.) Keep a well organized pack. It will make your camping experience much easier.

132.) Explore the other side of the mountain.

133.) Explore the next bend in the river.

134.) Explore the unknown trail.

135.) When exploring, always know your way home.

136.) Don't forget that wood off the ground will always be dryer than wood on the ground.

137.) Never say you're too young.

138.) Never head up the creek without a paddle.

139.) Be familiar with your gear before you need it.

140.) Don't forget to make certain that your backpack is adjusted to a comfortable fitting.

141.) Tolerate the bugs (chances are you've got no other alternative).

142.) Don't seal the lid on a bubbling sourdough crock pot.

143.) Always watch your campfire.

144.) Swap some stories with other people camping in the area.

145.) Never break wind in a
tent full of strangers.

146.) Put together an emergency repair kit for your equipment.

147.) Do not be afraid to don a poncho to hike in the rain from time to time.

148.) Never throw dirty dishwater into a river—except in designated river environments.

149.) Never sleep with food in bear country.

150.) Never underestimate the smaller critters either.

151.) Look at but don't touch the relics in places of ancestral importance.

152.) Romp around in the grass with bare feet.

153.) Make certain nothing in that grass will hurt your feet.

154.) For those chilly day rest breaks seek out sunny and wind-protected locations.

155.) Camp in a national park in the
dead of winter.

156.) Make certain you are not breaking any
park regulations by doing so.

157.) Keep your knife razor sharp.

158.) Don't be afraid to ignore the cooking instructions on trail food packages (it might be preferable to add twice as much water, and let it stand twice as long).

159.) Seam seal your tent.

160.) Don't climb mountains or boulders
that rise higher than your ability.

161.) Test your equipment before you trust it.

162.) Don't hike in a lightning/thunder storm.

163.) Never view nature as one would view television.

164.) Treat your camping equipment with respect.

165.) Do your dishes.

166.) Never believe that humans can eat whatever animals eat.

167.) Don't feed the animals; chances are they can't digest what we eat either.

168.) Don't portage barefoot.

169.) Try not to fill your camp stove any
more than three quarters of the
way full; there must be some
space for the tank to pressurize.

170.) Say hello to a passing hiker.

171.) Tread lightly.

172.) Don't wear all of your clothing inside your sleeping bag at night. Keep insulation in mind and utilize your dead air space.

173.) Pack as lightly as possible.

174.) Make sure your fire is out "COLD" when it is no longer in use.

175.) Never blow air into a self inflating sleeping pad when temperatures are below freezing. The moisture from your breath turns into ice.

176.) The road less traveled may make all the difference.

177.) Don't make the mistake
of believing that the
map is the country.

178.) Allow yourself plenty of time to set up camp in the winter months.

179.) Keep in mind that nature is not solely in the wilds, it's everywhere . . . it's a state of mind.

180.) Don't attempt to start a fire with logs as thick as your wrist.

181.) Don't make too many plans.
More often than not, the greatest
adventures will find you instead of you
having to find them.

182.) Make sure your camping permits
are visible.

183.) Always keep your sleeping gear
dry.

184.) Never lose your sense of respect for living things.

185.) Avoid perspiration in cold temperatures.

186.) Never think that a video camera is too much to carry, the extra weight is sometimes worth it.

187.) Never spill fuel on exposed flesh in sub-zero temperatures.

188.) Find who you are when you enter the wilderness.

189.) Hydration is key to life.

*—Buck Tilton*

190.) Silence is the heart of all great achievements. *—Buck Tilton*

191.) Never forget to call your contacts when your trip is concluded.

192.) Never judge a sleeping bag's warmth by its specified degree rating.

193.) Eat well to sleep warm.

194.) Camp out under the stars.

195.) Try building a sail for your canoe.

196.) Try to go on an extended campout at least once a year.

197.) You don't have to name plants
and animals. Their worth lies
beyond their label.

198.) Remember to unbuckle your waist belt, and sternum straps, when crossing streams.

199.) Choose complaints carefully when in the company of a large group.

200.) Clean your camping equipment after a campout.

201.) Don't leave open wounds (even small ones) untreated.

202.) Keep tents well ventilated to prevent moisture buildup.

203.) You cannot save time—you only choose how to spend it.

—*Buck Tilton*

204.) Learn at least some basic wilderness first aid.

205.) Create shapes from the clouds, but not while you're hiking over rough terrain with a heavy pack.

206.) Never pack store bought foods without first repackaging them.

207.) Try camping in all seasons.

208.) Remove a layer of clothing before you
sweat.               *—Buck Tilton*

209.) Learn CPR.

210.) Never pack heavy items in the
bottom of your pack.

211.) Find time to make-believe.

212.) Don't fall under the misconception that wool will keep you comfortable when wet. It has some insulating qualities; however, you will still be wet and uncomfortable.

213.) Never say you're too old.

214.) Learn how to make a cooking tripod.

215.) Never put soap in the food bag.

216.) Try camping for a weekend with as little as possible.

217.) Never take short cuts on
switch back trails.

218.) Never add fuel to a hot stove.

219.) Never believe that you are the ruler of all you survey.

220.) Don't underestimate the power of water when canoeing or kayaking.

221.) Never wash polypropylene in hot water unless you plan on letting a two year old wear it.

222.) Make certain your boots fit properly before hiking.

223.) Keep a journal.

224.) If no toilet paper is available, try wiping with snow.

225.) Always camp away from other campers.

226.) Learn to identify at least five constellations.

227.) If you aren't having fun, you're doing something wrong.

—*Buck Tilton*

228.) Remember to maximize your dead
     air space while insulating.

229.) Step to the music you hear, but not too
     loudly.

230.) Don't try to warm your booted feet
     by sticking them into the fire; you
     will only melt your boots.

231.) Don't believe that twenty pairs of socks will keep your feet warm.

232.) Don't always go hiking simply to see how many miles you can hike; enjoy the time while you have it.

233.) Never go on long hikes without a second pair of boot laces.

234.) Always expect the
unexpected in the bush.

235.) Take a snow shower.

236.) Make certain there is a warm cabin nearby afterwards.

237.) Don't always eat granola & rice bring some junk food.

238.) Never attempt to cook over blazing flames, low simmering coals work the best.

239.) Never show disrespect towards park officials. Dealing with the public is no meager task.

240.) Push yourself from time to time.

241.) Keep your center of gravity low and secure all gear properly when canoeing.

242.) Always look before you leap when jumping into a stream.

243.) Remember to prime your stoves in temperatures below 20 degrees.

244.) Don't wear gaudy neon colors in the bush; they just don't blend.

245.) Don't hesitate teaching others any skills you've acquired.

246.) Don't hesitate learning skills from others.

247.) Never go canoeing without an extra paddle.

248.) Always carry matches in a
waterproof container.

249.) Never go canoeing without a
sponge for mopping up "slosh"
water that comes into the canoe
over the gunwales.

250.) Never trust a wild animal.

251.) Be able to identify poison ivy, poison sumac, poison oak, and anything else poisonous for that matter.

252.) Never wash rain gear any more than necessary—sponge clean only.

253.) Know, or make an effort to learn the surrounding area in which you are camping.

254.) Don't buy an eight person tent for a two person job.

255.) The best looking gear is not always the best working gear.

256.) Remember, most hypothermia deaths occur between 30 and 50 degrees.

257.) Pay close attention to the weather.

258.) Before putting them on, check your boots for scorpions, when camping in the Southwest.

259.) Don't run camping stoves at full power. This will run down your stove, and waste your fuel.

260.) Never forget your manners. Just because you're in the bush doesn't mean you are at liberty to behave like a barbarian.

261.) Carry stove fuel in recommended containers and away from food.

262.) Never wash a sleeping bag in hot water.

263.) In order of importance: your companions, your gear, your destination.

264.) Cold feet can be rapidly warmed on someone's bare stomach. (It's better than frostbite.)

265.) Take time out to enjoy the power of a summer storm.

266.) Learn the basic canoe strokes.

267.) If possible, avoid setting up camp in open areas.

268.) Be humbled by the wilderness.

269.) Always break in new boots before hiking with them.

270.) Never tie yourself to a rope when crossing a river.

271.) Never, ever bring a
disobedient dog camping.

272.) When cooking freeze dried food in its bag, make sure you stir it well. If possible, pour it into another container.

273.) Make certain you are in good physical condition before you attempt any extreme hiking or climbing.

274.) Rediscover the magic of simple pleasures.

275.) Use potholders to prevent burnt fingers.

276.) Check your first aid kit to make sure nothing has expired.

277.) Periodically check yourself for ticks if they are in the area.

278.) Avoid crossing streams barefoot.

279.) If walking a great distance, try using a walking stick.

280.) The best place to test a backpack meal for taste is at home.

281.) Pack a designated bag for carrying out all of your garbage.

282.) Store sleeping bags in a day pack to use for side trips. —*Michael Hodgson*

283.) Always prepare for the
worst.

284.) Check your air mattress for leaks
before your trip.

285.) Lash any oddly shaped items to
the outside of your backpack.

286.) When camping, make a list of any
items you forgot to bring.

287.) Know how to use every item in your medical kit.

288.) Don't believe that alcohol will warm you up in cold weather.

289.) Wear loose-fitting clothing in hot temperatures.

290.) Keep a slow steady pace when
hiking at high altitudes.

291.) Always steer clear of avalanche
areas.

292.) Learn from your mistakes.

293.) Never filter water that is flowing under a dead moose. Find yourself a new watering hole!

# TO BRING, OR

# NOT TO BRING

*(that is the question!)*

## *NOTE*

The items listed in this half of the book are nothing more than a checklist of ideas. It will not be necessary to carry all of them, however you will find that some of these items pertain to most any camping situation.

I would suggest reading through the following list before your next camping adventure to see if perhaps you have left anything important behind. Just remember to keep your pack light, your mind open, and the wilderness clean. And, as always, have a great time.

## *NOTE*

The items listed in this half of the book are nothing more than personal opinions.  If you feel it absolutely necessary to bring any of these items, then by all means do so.  This is nothing more than a list of potential "back savers."  So, before you head out the door and into the world of wilderness, ask yourself that one critical question,
"Do I **really** need this?"
If your answer happens to be "no," leave it home.

However, as a common courtesy to your fellow campers, never bring the last three items mentioned in this book.

1.) Extra set of long underwear (no cotton).

2.) Extra pair of wool socks.

3.) Extra set of clothing.

4.) A tent that has no mosquito netting.

5.) A flashlight containing twelve "D" cell batteries.

6.) An alarm clock.

7.) Pita bread or tortillas (each stays fresh for up to ten days).

8.) Map.

9.) Compass.

10.) A chain saw for firewood.

11.) Lap top computers.

12.) The kitchen sink, in other words, pack light.

13.) "Strike-Anywhere" matches in a waterproof container.

14.) Extra pair of lightweight shoes or sandals for crossing rivers.

15.) Flavored drink crystals.

16.) A fifteen inch survival knife complete with a fold-out shot gun and global positioning satellite.

17.) Fifty pounds of camera equipment.

18.) A bad attitude.

19.) Sturdy zip-lock bags.

20.) Plenty of biodegradable toilet paper.

21.) Several of your favorite spices.

22.) Cotton clothing (I can't stress that enough).

23.) A portable television (definite NO-NO).

24.) An AM/FM radio.

25.) Rain parka and pants.

26.) Warm hat, or a hat that provides shade.

27.) Water filter.

28.) Grandma's cast iron skillet.

29.) The office (don't bring it to the outdoors, leave it where it belongs).

30.) Electric socks.

31.) Good sleeping pad.

32.) Good sleeping bag (make certain that it matches your camping climate).

33.) A tent that won't leak.

34.) A "Walkman."

35.) A sawed-off double barrel 12 gauge shotgun for anything that may go "bump" in the night.

36.) Canned food (unless you don't plan to hike very far).

37.) Small nip of rum to add to hot tea.

38.) Several packets of tea for your nip of rum.

39.) Sunglasses.

40.) Sunblock.

41.) A pocket knife that has more than ten blades. (Knives with 60 blades will only bruise your thigh while bouncing in your pocket.)

42.) A cat. No offense, but I've heard they make very poor camping companions. I, for one, wouldn't want to find out.

43.) First Aid Kit: (waterproof tape, 3" elastic bandage, sterile gauze pads, Neosporin, Spenco 2nd Skin, Spenco Adhesive Knit Bandage, elastic bandages, hydrocortisone cream, pain medication, anti-diarrheal medication, antacid tablets, splinter forceps.)

44.) Perfume, mousse, or styling spray. (Ladies, cosmetics will be a waste of your time when camping.)

45.) A copy of *The Wall Street Journal.*

46.) Electronic games.

47.) Foot powder.

48.) Your common sense.

49.) Some hard candy for the trail.

50.)   A hardcover novel consisting of
       over five thousand pages.

51.)   The wrong map.

52.)   A pillow . . . you'll survive.

53.)   Small flashlight, or headlamp.

54.)   <u>Razor</u> sharp knife.

55.)   A lightweight nesting cook kit.
        (Try scratching half-cup marks on
        the inside of your pots.)

56.) An economy size tube of tooth paste.

57.) A large can of mosquito spray; they do make small, concentrated bug repellents.

58.) Every camping gadget you own.

59.) Camera, film, and a set of extra batteries.

60.) Carry a bug jacket if heading north in the summer time.

61.) 50 feet of nylon parachute cord.

62.) An eighty-pound medical/survival kit if you will only be camping for a few days.

63.) A large lantern that outputs more candle power than the sun.

64.) A ten-pound fold-out grill.

65.)  A well-planned menu.  (Summer
      sausage, cheese, and crackers
      make an excellent trail lunch.)

66.)  COFFEE!  If you're a coffee fan,
      don't be caught dead without it.

67.)  A whistle.

68.) A twenty piece cook set if only you and a friend will be camping.

69.) A change of clothing for each and every day.

70.) A piece of gear that is on the verge of breaking.

71.) At least two wide mouth plastic bottles.

72.) Sturdy plastic utensils (metal weighs too much).

73.) Biodegradable soap.

74.)  A metal canteen.

75.)  A water filter that has become
      dirty or clogged.

76.)  Ten Sunday newspapers for
      starting campfires.

77.) A compact stove if fires are not permitted in the area.

78.) Plenty of fuel for your stove.

79.) Small repair kit for your stove, tent, and backpack.

80.) Jewelry; it becomes lost too easily.

81.) An instrument that you can't play, unless embarking on a solo journey.

82.) A cast iron dutch oven.

83.) Compact survival kit: 70 feet of
fishing line, several fish hooks,
strike anywhere matches, tablets
to disinfect water, sharp knife,
metal cup for boiling water, signal
mirror, candles, emergency
blanket, and 50 feet of strong
nylon parachute cord.

84.)    A pager.

85.)    A cellular phone.

86.)    A briefcase.

ICS BOOKS is offering YOU, the reader of this book the chance to have your own camp lore, camping tips, and humor published by ICS BOOKS some time in the future.
Just send your quips to ICS BOOKS, Inc. PO Box 10767, Merrillville IN. 46411-0767

Send a type written copy of any tips, camp lore, and humor stating your name, address, the date, and phone number.

The permission line must state that none of the submitted entries have been previously printed or published in any form, electronic or mechanical; including recorded broadcasts. Sign and date each entry.

ICS BOOKS will print your name somewhere in the book stating you are the originator of the quip you submit.

ICS BOOKS retains the right to edit or change any quip submitted without written permission from the originator.